Get the Interview Get the Job:
How to Get Standout Resume Success and Interview Results

By

Matthew P Dovell

Table of Contents:

Part I Get the Interview:

Get the Interview Introduction	Page 5
Prologue	Pages 6-7
Chapter One: The Job Search	Pages 8-18
Chapter Two: The Application	Pages 19-20
Chapter Three: Selling Yourself	Pages 21-27
Chapter Four: The Cover Letter	Page 28-29
Chapter Five: The Resume	Pages 30-37
Conclusion	Page 37
Resume Examples	Pages 38
Bad Resumes	Pages 39-47
Good Resumes	Pages 48-52
Better Resumes	Pages 53-74

Part II Get the Job:

Introduction	Page 75
Prologue	Page 76
The Interview	Pages 77-88
Conclusion	Pages 89-91

Author's Note
(c)Copyright 2018 by Matthew P Dovell - All rights reserved.

This document is geared towards providing exact and reliable information in regards to the topic and issue covered. The publication is sold with the idea that the publisher is not required to render accounting, officially permitted, or otherwise, qualified services. If advice is necessary, legal or professional a practiced individual in the profession should be ordered.

From a Declaration of Principles which was accepted and approved equally by a Committee of the American Bar Association and a Committee of Publishers and Associations.

In no way is it legal to reproduce, duplicate or transit any part of this document in either electronic means or in printed format. Recording of this publication is strictly prohibited and any storage of this document is not allowed unless with written permission from the publisher. All Rights reserved.

The information provided herein is stated to be truthful and consistent, in that any liability, in terms of inattention or otherwise, by any usage or abuse of any policies, processes, or directions contained within is the solitary and utter responsibility of the recipient reader. Under no circumstances will any legal responsibility or blame be held against the publisher for any reparatio, damages, or monetary loss due to the information herein, either directly or indirectly.

Respective authors own all copyrights not held by the publisher.

The information herein is offered for informational purposes solely, and is universal as so. The presentation of the information is without contract or any type of guarantee assurance.

The trademarks that are used are without consent and the publication of the trademark is without permission or baking by the trademark owner. All trademarks and brands within this book are for clarifying purposes only and are owned by the owners themselves, not affiliated with this document.

Any websites and/or products mentioned in the context of this book are being made as a recommendation only. No financial compensation or endorsement has been solicited to the author by any of the respective owners or manufactures thereof.

Introduction:

You want better things in life but do not know where to go. The economy is improving but your employer either is not providing much for advancement and/or raises. You *think* need a new job. But more importantly how do you do that and where do you go? Where do you start and how should this work? Maybe you not been searching for a job in a while. Yes, the economy has improved but that does not mean that the process has changed. Get the Interview provides you with solid advice on how to find opportunities and create a knock them out resume that will get you the interview. This book is catered to young adults as well as seasoned professionals that might be looking to change paths.

Prologue

If you are reading this book I take it you are looking for work and assistance in resume skills. Before we get to the major topics at hand let me address a few things. First employers are *not* charities; no one is specifically forced to hire anyone. Even with the economy being what it is the job process can be grueling and frankly to be blunt not fun. It takes significant time, money and energy to hire people. Secondly is that this is *not* some inspirational or self-help book. If you are looking for that stop reading this book and get that one. This book is not mean to be your stereotypical business trend book and I am not spinning pie plates. Sound practical and relevant advice is the name of the game here. It was said by President Ronald Reagan long ago that "The best social program is a job." Even if you are currently working there is still the chance that there are better opportunities out there.

This book is to provide accurate and timely advice to help people find opportunities. This book unlike some of the others of this subject on Kindle is not ghostwritten. I stand by its content. From the 2008 recession and its aftermath, I applied to quite a number of positions and found out what employers look for and what they do not. My academics, certifications, volunteering and work experience helped solidify the advice provided herein. This book also examines useful websites to use as tools as well as real-world examples usually from government and political perspectives. Resume writing is not fun but it is part of the process regardless of where you are in your career. You also must put yourself in the hiring manager's shoes as you have to see yourself as they see you. What matters most to them is that they see you as one of them in the role of what they want. If you cannot convince them of that then you probably will not get the interview and certainly will not get the job.

Lastly to note is that this book is written strictly from a perspective within the United States There can be significant differences in the way how resumes, cover letters and the interview process works in other countries. These differences can actually be considered discrimination if not be outright illegal (such as mandating photographs with resumes). If you are outside of the United States and have application questions please consult that organizations human resources department.

Chapter One: The Job Search

Media advertising has changed significantly in the past twenty years. In a world with declines in traditional media advertising employment opportunities is now largely online. The era of the large Sunday newspaper filled with a huge full-color employment or help wanted section is long gone. Employer websites vary dramatically in how they treat their applicants. There are some I have seen that had a complete archive going back years while at the same point others that delete the posting immediately upon its application date. Some websites have RSS feeds or email lists that you can receive new openings. Although that is good that comes to cost to them and frankly if they have a tight budget that might not always be an option. There might also be delays depending on schedule. I will teach you the secrets of making this system more efficient and effective.

One of the greatest tips that I can provide is to use change detection and notification (CDN) systems such as Visual Ping, Change Detect, Internet Owl, Website Watcher and Google Alerts. These systems can provide an alert when page updates *and* can often show you specifically what specifically was added and removed. Why would this be useful? Consider the following:

- Did the posted salary change? If so is it still appealing?
- Did the application period move (earlier or later)? The earlier you apply the better but if it was moved later that could be later starting date.
- Did the status of it change (full time, part time, seasonal etc.) This has can have a direct impact on benefits, pay attention.
- Did the requirements change? This should not happen but

- Did the funding of it change (operating to grants or vice versa)? Grants are nearly always temporary and have little wiggle room for negotiations.
- Did the status change (exempt to nonexempt or vice versa)? Is this salary or hourly? This definition along with responsibilities is a very significant discussion these days.

I have utilized ChangeDetection (the precursor of Visual Ping) for practically six years and it informs when the alert was started, when it was last changed and when was the last sizeable change. These systems vary anywhere from free to paid models depending on how wide of a range you want to search and how frequently you want to check. I would advise you to use these systems on your own time for a variety of reasons. First looking for a job on work time is not advisable and second in some cases these systems can have a false read as a proxy avoidance system and thus are blocked.

Here is a step by step way to use Visual Ping:
1) Go to visualping.io and register.

2) Login and go to create a new job.

3) From there put in the website that you want to monitor. You can have it checked at 5, 30 or 60 minutes, every day or weekly.

4) Then select what email address to send the results. Lastly with advanced you can select visual or web. Visual means you will click on the site to find an area where it changes whereas web is based on the text. Tiny change, medium or major.

5) Then you can give the search a name. This helps when you do get results.

Generally the more services you want the more it will cost but there are free services.

The free policy can make two checks a day or 62 a month, for $4 monthly is 10 checks a day or 313 a month, $13 is 40 checks/1200 a month, $24 is 130 checks/4000 a month and $58 is 333 checks a day /10,000 a month.

Another one is Versionista.com which is much the same concept. Five sites checked a day for free or 150 checks a month. $99 a month for 600 checks etc. The objective with these is to save time rather than trying to remember what a site was at given time. If you use Chrome as a browser there is an app called Page Monitor that can be as small as one click for monitoring.

Here is a step by state way to use Google Alerts. This is a more broad approach but can provide information.
1) Get a google account and go to www.google.com/alerts
2) Type in what topic or subject you want to monitor.
3) You can pick frequency (as it happens, daily weekly), sources (automatic, news, blogs, web, books, video, discussion etc.)
4) Click the option area and select Delivery time or Digest. Delivery time allows you to set what time of day you want to receive an alert. Digest on the other hand allows you to send the notice to anyone and pick a daily or weekly digest

Having information that is catered for you on your own terms can be a great assistance. Also, keep in mind sometimes these systems can have the ability to look *backward*. Knowing what they did in the past can give good indications when other people were hired and the

10

general ebb and flow. Since these are largely automatic they operate 24/7 it becomes a passive activity. If you have ever read Tim Ferris's Four Hour Work Week you might have some idea of this type of process. I would also recommend examining any information about the organization itself. Websites and press releases are a given but try digging deeper into budget documents, agendas and minutes if you can find them. Keep in mind news is reported fast and happens fast. During an interview, I mentioned how I keep up and read their local news. He then responded "So then you know I am leaving in two weeks!" Try using LinkedIn to find the backgrounds of those that might be your boss and coworkers. Knowing more about their backgrounds and what is going on would provide a better experience during the interview. Just keep in mind your profile views are notified to them as well unless you change your preferences.

You can find more about a position if you work a bit backward. Recently I was sent an email from a significant non profit that mentioned an opening checking their website I did not see a current employee with that title. However, in using Google Advanced Search I found a position very close to that with a different title. Using Google Advanced Search allows you to search within a domain name to find content that might not immediately come to the surface. Direct hyperlinks might have been removed but content tends to stay. The standards for the first job were of seven to ten years' experience while the newer posting says five. The older posting listed a salary and the newer one did not. From there I looked on LinkedIn to search for people within the employer. There I could find the prior employee and how long it took between that person leaving and the new job posted. This again provides an advantage in knowing what the prior employees brought to the position, especially with the private sector.

In terms of finding more opportunities, there are many trade associations. Some believe the decline of unions led to a decline in industry group influence. Nothing could be further from the truth. Think about a profession. Now think about what it does, what it does it for and a location. Just off the top of my head I searched for a number of professions with locations and low and behold they exist. Here are just a few examples:

- Iowa Society of Certified Public Accountants (www.iacpa.org)
- Reno-Tahoe Chapter of American Marketing Association (www.renoama.com)
- Louisiana Collision Industry Association (www.la-cia.com)
- Maine Water Environment Association (www.mewea.org)
- Georgia Association of Realtors (www.garealtor.com)
- Oregon Society of Soil Scientists (www.oregonsoils.org)

Trade associations represent people that work within an industry. Some are stronger than others but generally they get together to form better standards, notify each other of job opportunities and of course lobby government. Often times these organizations write the book (sometimes literally!) on regulations and are more apt to know about new opportunities. The newsletters and archives that these provisions provide can become valuable tools to see how the industry is doing. Some of these also have subdivisions and may have groups based on scalability. Major populated areas probably have local organizations (New

York City, Chicago, Los Angeles etc.) and then there are state and national affiliates.

Here is another major tip that can make you stand out from the crowd. *If these organizations have any forms of certifications or courses, by all means, take them.* In many respects, such classes can be considered obscure and potentially very specific. However, these are so specifically detailed that the validity is there. These can cost as little as tens of dollars up to thousands. Now to be fair certifications are not specifically advertised as an employment tool but they without question show effort. Training is often seen as an issue as employers continue to argue about the "skills gap".

Here are a few examples of training certification:

- Certified Fraud Examiner - www.acfe.com
- Certified Professional Marketer - www.ama.org/events-training/certification/pages/digital-marketing-certificaiton.aspx
- American Translator Association Certification - www.atanet.org/certification/
- National Property Management Association Certification - www.npma.org/?Certification
- Association of Energy Engineers - Certifications www.aeecenter.org/certifications
- Association of Record for Bid, Proposal, Business Development, Capture, and Graphics Professionals www.apmp.org/?page=AccreditationProgram

In a market where we often hear about noncompetitive clauses and non-disclosure agreements, such programs can make a huge difference for job applicants. Remember that they will know *exactly* what these accomplishments mean.

The old saying of "How do you get a job without the experience and how do you get the experience without the job?" is shattered by this. You are speaking their language and they will notice. Think about what happens to a resume that has something of the above versus one that does not.

Hiring Manager: "Ok this one has a bachelor's degree, four years' experience"

Hiring Manager Assistant: "This one has a bachelor, two years' experience but *just* earned our certification last year!"

Hiring Manager: "They must be *really* serious about this job if they went through that seminar. They only offer that twice a year, it is tested *and* I probably know people that were there."

Who do you think they will choose to interview over the other? Of course, it will be the latter of the two. This is by no means to belittle experience but many of these certifications are tested and not everyone passes them.

In addition to certifications, employers often have niches of software suites and standards. These are not generally commercially available to the general public. In the private sector, examples are Six Sigma, Kaizen, or ISO 9000. With nonprofits, they might be using the form of the fundraising software Raiser's Edge. Within the public sector, the use of Tyler Technology products such as MUNIS would also fill this role. Learning to use these tools can play an important role in giving an advantage. The more you appear to be one of their employees the higher the likelihood that they will interview you. The only caveat with this is to make sure that you still stay current with any trends. You will hear sometimes about the number of continuing education units (CEU's) that must be maintained to keep yourself in status. Some organizations might require tests and certain amounts of classroom time. If you are really on a low budget for training classes some of these might have video content online on sites like Youtube but again you should check the age of content and if it was actually them that uploaded it.

Remember that it helps to think not just where a job is a today but also a year, five years, ten years down the line. How many photographs have you developed in the past ten to fifteen years? How secure did Kodak and Polaroid look in the 1990s? How many floppy disks have you used in the past twenty years? Where is Radio Shack today? How many administrative assistants do you see in an era of Siri, Google, Cortina and Alexa? The point being is that it can be hard to predict where technological change and displacement can occur. We have also seen various corporate scandals in the past eighteen years where many people were let go to no fault of their own. Your skills are yours and you should be able to apply them and build upon them in your career. Do not let one employer dictate how far you can go.

Make no mistake there are some industries and professions that do not attract the same number of applicants. Some applicants might be intimidated by working in an area that differs from what they are used to. It could be too urban-rural or remote, too large in staffing/bureaucracy, too small etc. When applying for a job you usually do not know what their applicant pool looks like. Having said that though you want to cater an application and resume specifically towards that employer. Otherwise, you are going to end up emphasizing things that are not relevant and deemphasizing things that are relevant. This may be frustrating to some but if employers speak to each other about applicants and see the same materials it can cheapen your personal image.

With the public sector and to a lesser degree nonprofit are pretty open with their information. Finding vital statistics such as budgets, staffing, and organizational structure is relatively simple. With the private sector, it is not always as open. One tip I can recommend is to use Google Advanced to search within a domain name and you can sometimes find internal documents. You can type in other forms of file extensions. Office based ones work the best .doc, xls, .pdf etc. In addition, private companies can issue Request for Proposals (RFP) that can allude to future employment activity. Years ago, Amazon advertised for openings in southeastern Massachusetts. Their nearest facility at the time was in Nashua New Hampshire. About a week later Amazon announced plans for their current facility in Stoughton Massachusetts.

There can be intimidation against applying for positions but keep in mind it cannot hurt to just apply. You do not know what the other applicants might have. Remember hiring can be like negotiations one party will go higher and the other lower and eventually meet in the middle. This is why there are differences between job qualifications and what is outright settled for a qualified candidate. In short, there are asking prices and selling prices.

Sometimes I find that there is a mentality of people dismissing positions for three reasons:

- The position requires some form of education, training, experience, and certification,
- They are not hiring enough people.
- The pay and benefits are too low.

These mentalities focus on positions that are easy to get, employ a large number of people and have high compensation. In many respects this is contradictory. If many people can do the same job it will have *less* security and compensation, not more. If a position does not require some form of education, experience, training or a certification chances are it does not pay well. The fact of the matter for those that are younger and have less experience you have to start somewhere. Being employed in at itself helps with networking and provides experience. This is not to suggest that you should accept anything but you do have to keep in mind that the longer you may be out of the job market the harder it will be. To note if you find yourself in a noncompetitive agreement and unemployed I would highly suggest consulting a labor attorney and checking any state/province and local laws. It would be hard to argue that someone cannot be hired by competition as they have value while at the same time they do not present a value to their current employer.

Worksheet

Change Notify Detection List

- ☐ Subject _____
- ☐ Frequency_____
- ☐ Delivery or Digest? _____

- ☐ Subject _____
- ☐ Frequency_____
- ☐ Delivery or Digest? _____

- ☐ Subject _____
- ☐ Frequency_____
- ☐ Delivery or Digest? _____

Trade Associations:

- ☐ Location _____
- ☐ Association _____
- ☐ Profession _____
- ☐ Is there a newsletter? _____
- ☐ What issues are there currently? _____
  _____

- ☐ Location _____
- ☐ Association _____
- ☐ Profession _____
- ☐ Is there a newsletter? _____
- ☐ What issues are there currently? _____
  _____

Chapter Two: The Application

Answer all questions truthfully but please remember that not all employers are on the same page of what can be asked. There is one employer I know of that was photocopying their application from the same template they bought back in the late 1970's. Needless to say, there were several questions on it that legally cannot be asked today, at least in the United States. Here are some examples. The first two were actually on that application.

- Are you married?
- Have you ever been sick for more than a month?
- Are you a US Citizen? - Not required but there are no legal mandates to sponsor visas
- What is your native tongue/language? - To note there are some ESL jobs that *do* require this.
- How old are you?
- When do you plan to retire?
- Do you plan to have children?
- Do you have children or will want to have children?
- What are your height and weight? - If the position has safety requirements with this it would be up to the employee to judge if they are in compliance.
- Do you smoke or drink? – They can test after accidents.
- Anything involving a protected class. - Race, color, religion, gender and natural origin are protected by the Civil Rights Act of 1964
- Do you have any mental or physical disabilities? – Americans with Disabilities Act makes this unlawful.
- Questions on military service. This is a federally protected class.

Applications might also ask for references, letters of recommendation and writing samples. References are straightforward enough. Keep in mind that if you flag someone prior to not be contacted that might be construed as odd. No one realistically is going to give a bad reference so these days this is standard boilerplate. With an actual letter of recommendation remember that there should be some highlights of accomplishment and relationships that you made. Also, the older a recommendation letter is the more difficult it will be to use. If you are relying on ones that are a decade old they could be dismissed. Try focusing on current employers, known colleagues and perhaps a place you volunteered or interned at. Writing samples, on the other hand, might be focused more on prior academic work or publishing.

Chapter Three: Selling Yourself

Social media cannot be ignored in selling yourself. You should consider how you view to others online in a variety of formats If there are readers that are involved in nonprofits keep in mind that if you are involved in those that are political it is considered as a reflection of yourself to a human resources manager. For example, on LinkedIn, I found a few people that have volunteered or worked for such a number of nonprofits that it clearly indicated a line of thought. That might be good if that is the intention for the future but not always. Let me illustrate a few examples:

- A man who has connections to Ralph Naders PIRG groups, animal welfare/liberation groups that can be described by some as left wing. He is located in Michigan (not Detroit)
- A Ph.D. candidate who is involved in secular humanist activities and actually had a photo of himself with Richard Dawkins. He was in the Atlanta Georgia area.

In each case, the person has activities that go against the grain politically of the surrounding area. This is not to suggest that you must repress any passionate issues but if it is viewed politically it can become a turnoff to employers. If you must volunteer or be involved with a nonprofit try to find one that is apolitical as possible to lower any controversy. In short if the job description says you are to be an activist by all means do but if not, do not.

LinkedIn can be an extremely good tool to use especially in the private sector. At first, I hated LinkedIn for about a month because I could not make heads or tails out of it. Gradually I learned to like it as it grew. When you think about connections think of any place you worked at, went for your education, volunteered, friends, relatives etc.

Another network secret to gain connections is to look for those that are in the arts industry and thanking them for their work. Painters, musicians, authors, people in television or radio production and even computer/app programmers are not often thanked for their contributions specifically. Take the time to look up the credits and reach out you might be surprised. Joining groups or looking for groups that you already belong to is another great way to gain connections. It can be intimidating to try to ask people questions that you might not have in common with. But if you have a few more connections in common they will be more apt to reply.

Needless to say, with social media you can also be judged on what others might say. Websites like Scrubber.Social can scan your online profiles and allow you to edit anything that may appear offensive. If all it takes is one bad Tweet on Twitter or a Facebook post to put you in a rejected pile this might be well worth it. Having used some similar programs in the past there can be false reads but it is much faster to use programs rather than to manually go back months if not potentially years or even a decade. A general rule of thumb to consider is this. <u>If you think it is offensive it probably is</u>. Anything racist, sexist, misogynistic, homophobic, bigoted, ageist, militant etc. should be avoided. Many employers have social media policies that can actually discipline up to the point of termination depending on what was posted. Please consult human resources policies for more exact specifics.

If you are looking to add to your reputation in a connecting way I would suggest checking out Help a Reporter Out - HARO. <u>www.helpareporterout.com</u> HARO sends out at least one email a day from news organizations looking for experts on subjects. These vary dramatically but the advantage is this cost just a few emails. Reporters do not always have the time or the budget to find an expert. Being quoted can gradually compound and provide backup to your online reputation. Reporters look for responses usually within a few days and vary from blogs to major news outlets. There is no assurance that you would be quoted but being quoted can provide credibility in a unique way.

How you sell yourself in the interview process deals with framing. Remember that each organization and department have their own functions and purpose. *What is a priority to one is not always a priority to another.* Your body is made up of different systems that work together for different purposes in order for you to live. Likewise, the same is for employers. Put yourself in their shoes and consider how *they* see you. Say you have a project and they want you to see it to completion from beginning to end. I would recommend viewing things in the following frames: Managerial, Political, Legal, Efficiency, and Results. Let us examine this in order.

Think about what it means to be a manager. What is expected for work within a given week, month and year? What is expected from results? How should the workflow in the year? Does it have an expected predictability?

Political might not be as measured specifically but looking at the relationship *between* departments. What would you consider to be an order of operations should someone be out? In terms of governance how much would be told to a board (shareholders, directors, public officials?). How should succession planning and lateral transfers work? Before you ask another department to do something what do they need from you in order to do it?

That leads us to the legal perspective of what legally has to be provided. Compliances with regulations are not something to be taken lightly. This gets to what writer Mary Parker Follett argued in The Giving of Orders that people work better responding to a situation rather than a general command. General commands can be taken personally and be depersonalizing it they are more likely to be obeyed.

For legalities, you do not ever want to tell anyone to do things that are illegal. That also means you have to check if things are being done legally. This can deal with say auditing time records to ensure that people are not working off clock, the accuracy of safety and financial records.

There are situations where results are geared towards efficiency versus results. As long as a document is legible and able to be reproduced that is all that is required. The last I checked no one has ever sold artwork out of a fax machine! Results only situations are to the point. An example of that can be food allergies. If the meal is to be 100% peanut free there is really no room for error. Food allergies can cause sickness and in extreme cases death.

It also helps to sell yourself as someone that can see through the course of time. Having the ability to plan shows an ability to take control and manage. Regardless of what management style you use if you get questioned chances are you will be asked why you reached such an action and how you got to that point.

If you recently graduated higher education or high school you should reconsider what you have put online. According to a survey by Career Builder in 2017 70% of employers use social media to screen job applicants before hiring. What should you consider removing? The following is some of what the survey found that resulted in them *not* hiring a candidate:

- Positing provocative information
- Using drugs or drinking
- Racist, Sexist or bigoted
- Criminal behavior
- Sharing confidential data of employers and employees
- Lying about taking time off
- Lying about qualifications
- Poor Grammar/interactions

Now does this mean you simply unregister and unplug from everything? No not at all. In fact that might actually make things worse. They might think something is up if you have absolutely nothing to show. Employers do not want surprises after the fact. So what does look good? Any achievement on paper should be scanned. Degrees, certifications, licenses, how about a news article of where you work, anywhere you have been quoted or published etc. Much of this is going to compound with time it will get better.

For those that are of an older generation say forty and up here are some ways to manage social media. Remember like a resume social media can be a commodity. Although there is nothing bad about being photographed having a drink as an adult if all of the photos are of cats or kids that might not be that attractive. Just because someone has children in at itself does not mean they are a top candidate for a job.

The website "If This Then That" is a product that can automate social media. It can create automation and connections between websites like Facebook, LinkedIn and Google and at the same time between platforms like Apple and Android. Being able to automate social media can save significant amounts of time. The next page shows several IFTTT useful applets.

Remember in the past when there was breaking news and it got to the point? I have used one of these for RSS feed updates to my tablet. If the news article looks good I can swipe it and read, if not just ignore. High speed internet, portability with tablets and phones and social media are all great but sometimes it takes so much attention away that it slows your productivity. Products like If This Then That help filter out distractions that might otherwise bog us down. Social media platforms are doing the same things so it saves time if photos and text updates are the same. Remember we should be able to control social media. It should *not* be able to control you.

To note if you must eliminate a profile you can post a note that says something to the effect that "This profile will no longer be updated. Go to _____ for current content and to communicate". That gets to the point and lets employers know to look at other areas.

If This Then That (IFTTT) Applets

Save liked tweets to a Google Spreadsheet
https://ifttt.com/applets/113241p-save-the-tweets-you-like-on-twitter-to-a-google-spreadsheet

Automatically archive texts you send from your Android Phone to Google drive
https://ifttt.com/applets/mSV7cRrq-automatically-back-up-new-texts-you-receive-on-your-android-device-to-a-google-spreadsheet

Keep your Facebook and twitter profiles in sync. This updates your twitter photo when your Facebook photo is updated
https://ifttt.com/applets/8981p-keep-your-facebook-and-twitter-profile-pictures-in-sync

When a text message is sent, save it to a Google Drive document (each gets its own doc)
https://ifttt.com/applets/386326p-when-a-sms-is-sent-save-it-to-a-google-drive-document-each-contact-gets-its-own-doc?s=era2

When you are tagged in a Facebook photo you will receive an email with it attached.
https://ifttt.com/applets/57047p-when-you-re-tagged-in-a-pic-on-facebook-you-will-receive-an-email-with-it-attached?s=era2

Save email attachments to Google Drive
https://ifttt.com/applets/ESeruKXp-save-new-email-attachments-from-gmail-to-google-drive

Chapter Four: The Cover Letter

Gradually cover letters have become a bit of an iffy thing. They have faded with time but it can be argued are still needed in today's day and age. A cover letter should be able to provide an introduction and purpose to who you are and provide a backstory of why this is the "next step" for you. You want to touch on prior experience but it is not limited to just experience on the job. If you can prove with citing regulations with what the employer is looking for that can be an asset.

You should feed the job description back to the cover letter. This proves that you read it and you understand what they are asking for. As long as you have the credentials asked you can cite them. For example, if the job is for a distribution manager at a grocery chain you can cite the specific size of the buildings you worked with and the wide range of products, you can cite the number of employees managed, you can site safety regulations you complied with etc. Take the time to look up names and titles. "To whom it may concern" or "Human Resource Manager" is not a good idea. You would not respond to someone calling you by your job title, would you? Likewise, address them as you would in any formal letter. Again, cover letters are a bit on their way out but at the same point, it does show more effort and possibly leads to a higher likelihood that the resume would be read. The next page is a cover letter example.

Your Address
Attn:(Job title – Remember it is *their* role)or Mr/Mrs/Ms
Organization Name/division (get as specific as you can)
Address

Re: (The position you are applying for)

Dear (same name as above)

As a [insert academics or job role] with years of [apply experience], I am qualified to contribute to the [org name] [efforts to describe job]. Please consider me for the [job]

Recently as the _____ at _____I utilized (describe what you currently do). I also (describe another task you do at work)

Prior to that as [title and place – employer/internship etc.], I [explain what you did as above]. I also [name another task at the other place, make sure that t

In the [employer/internship/volunteering etc.] my experiences have varied from [pick to or three different tasks]. In addition I have experience working [relate this with regulations, research and development, sales records, management of people, budgets, space etc. Show an emphasis in *exact* terms)

As a [emphasize professionalization of what you do] I am well aware of the challenges that [orgs] in the region face. My experiences in working as (reference again the above in titles) makes me the ideal candidate for this position.

I would like to speak with you further in an interview if possible. I can be reached at (555-555-1212) or via email at (email) Thank you for your time and consideration. Sincerely,
(Name)

Chapter Five: The Resume

What much of this chapter deals with is the use of language. This is not to refer to your native language. This is about being able to document terminology in both written and verbal forms to create a common bond that makes you become attractive to an employer.

You should always consider what you did *relative* to your organization. Often times we lose track of what we are really doing in the importance that it has relative to work. What I mean by that is you need to take a look at each and every aspect of what you do. Are you working within a business cycle, what is the standard operating procedure, what government regulations do you work with, what industry standards do you work with etc.

Some of this might take you back to third and fourth grade English class but the more specific and better it sounds the better. Keep in mind there is what you do and what you do it for. Let me take a job I had for a kid as an example. The job itself involved manually counting votes for companies. Eventually, this was automated to Pitney Bowes machines and then simply 1-800 numbers and email. To describe it would be to show a gradual evolution.

Version 1
Flipped pages into piles. -- This does not say anything at all

Version 2
Sorted financial pages for a company. -- Slight improvement but tell us more

Version 3
Tabulated proxies for mutual fund companies. -- States exactly what it was.

Say as much as what you can with as few words as possible. You do not have to be a member of Toastmasters to understand that you are judged by the words of which you use. Do not assume that someone knows you. It is not an insult to explain yourself. Keep in mind your audience and <u>you should always consider that your resume is prime real estate</u>. I cannot emphasize this enough. If there is anything that you believe that does not contribute in any way shape form or regard to getting your interview take it off. I actually met someone who states on her LinkedIn profile that she made dean's list while at a community college in 1982! No offense to her but such an achievement more than thirty five years later is not something that needs to take up space to show an impact with an employer. A resume is not to be a complete A to Z examination of who you are. That is curriculum vitae and generally highlights accomplishments going well beyond with most hiring managers are willing to read let alone evaluate. While there are some positions that do require that, this book is predominantly focused on a resume of one to two pages at most. If you must illustrate more consider leaving a note at the end leading to a web address for a full CV and/or other material.

At the very least you want to make sure there are no typographical errors. Although misspellings are easy to find grammar differs from spelling. In addition you want to consider the formatting. Repeating a bit from above how much of your resume is significantly empty white space? Using justify helps make descriptions fill up the whole page rather than aligning to the left. Centering an be fine for headings but it is not for descriptions. Some will even judge an email address. Use an email address of your service provider or a free service such as GMail. If you use one that emphasizes a prior employer they might be reluctant to respond. If your email reflects some club or activity of the past use another. If it looks even *remotely* like Mike@dungeons&dragonsclubofHartford.com or sexylonglasheslisa@aol.com you need to change use something else!

A pet peeve of mine has always been when people sell themselves short. You might actually know more than you think you know if you take a step back and start looking up more specific terms. Here is an example. Where you currently work do they tend to manage by accomplishments? If so that is really called "Management by Objective". It was actually coined long ago by management guru Peter Drucker in his 1954 book The Practice of Management. Did your supervisor ever have you manually inspect operations by walking around? That is a term called Management by Walking around which started at Hewlett Packard in the 1970's. Have you ever managed inventory or sales? There are different methods such as Last in First out (LIFO) and First in First out (FIFO). Take what are normal business operations and look up what are related methods: finance, inventory/asset management, human resources, planning, merger and acquisition and purchasing. Chances are you might actually have been following terms of business, accounting, finance, marketing and planning without even knowing it. Remember the movie Karate Kid? "Wax on, Wax off" became useful later in the tournament. How about Slumdog Millionaire? The host could not believe he knew the answers to the questions due to his background but his experiences proved otherwise. Look up what the employer uses and apply as much as what you can to what they do.

When you send your resume, make sure to save the file as a PDF. PDF as a file format is ironclad. If you send a Microsoft Word file there is no real assurance that it will appear the same to the person receiving it. If their version of Word does not contain the exact same fonts and font sizes it will reformat your resume to different defaults and cause it look considerably different. Long ago I attended a job fair and did not have paper copies of my resume. I went to their business area and tried to print mine out but the Word version was different. It grew from two pages to three. The formatting, fonts, and sizing were totally incorrect and it looked horrific. That is too much of a risk to take in an application process. If you do attend job fairs bring resumes on paper ahead of time or email it to them.

The best advice that I was personally provided for resumes is that *you must consider them to be a spreadsheet with words*. People see things with sizes and numbers. Let us use the example of real estate. What was the average square footage of what you sold? How large were the land plots? How big was your staff? How big was your budget? Did you deal with significant market upturns and downturns? Every employer has a story. Did you work at a startup and face competition from day one? Did you navigate a significant merger or buyout? Questions like these are more open-ended but it can show a story and how you reacted. In a nutshell, they want to see if you are paying attention.

You should also not name drop but regulations and policy drop. That shows you know more about the technical knowledge. This is especially good if this new position uses current terms. Name dropping does not help because if they wanted names chances are you already gave them that in the form of a letter of recommendation. You do not want it to look as if you are being hired for anything other than your own merits. Furthermore, in the public and nonprofit sectors (and increasingly in private), it is not that hard to find out who does what. The idea that somehow this is secret and by itself has value just is not the case these days. Simply knowing someone should never be considered a qualification for employment.

Remember when you apply you really have just one shot at this. Most employers do not allow you take back applications or resumes to adjust. There are some websites that might allow you to save an application and send it. Remember to get some confirmation that they actually received it in the form of a sent email or confirmation screen. Long ago a person reached out to me for a resume critique and he did something very specific, he put a QR code on it. Now in the IT industry that he works in that might be perfectly fine. Outside of that, it could appear to be something very strange. I told him to flat out that if he used it outside of the IT industry it would be an immediate turnoff. You may have heard of the applicant that sent a shoe in a box with an application and a note saying "I already have one foot in the door". Gimmicks do not work. Standing out just to the point of standing out does not create value. If you could learn to type by flipping a keyboard upside down that would stand out but it would still just be the ability to type. Comedian Chris Rock once joked that "You can try to drive a car with your feet but that does not make it right!" Likewise, quantify what you know in a method that they can understand. There are no magic words or handshakes that can increase your odds.

A good product to use with resumes is the website jobscan.co. It compares a resume to a job description and shows what are the most common and uncommon matches. Another good site is diffnow. Diffnow allows you to put up two documents and side by side find out what is common and uncommon. It acts more like a computer program versus jobscan but it can handle many different file formats. If you can phrase accomplishments in different ways and apply it that can help makes it past some of the screening software.

Remember when human resource managers hire it is not like they take seventy or so resumes, put them on a desk and have a few department heads pick it over. Some people *actually* believe this. It flat out is not true. They look for keywords, language, and numbers. If you do not say or at least infer it then they cannot assume it. What many people hate about online applications processes is that they believe their resume gets lost, accidentally deleted, the process takes too long and it is little if any follow-up. It should be said that from an employer perspective hiring can take a long time just to establish the basics. When I was in the job market there was one employer that immediately emailed me back about the process. He informed me he was expecting eighty applicants. He received *one hundred eighty applications*. He then mentioned he was going to cull it down to twenty-five, then phone interview of 12 and second interview of six. To mail or email out a rejection notice to everyone can be taxing especially if there are replies asking why they did not get chosen for an interview. Employers are not career coaches and frankly, do not have the time to sit down and go line by line about what you should have detailed.

Chances are what happens is they have someone codify what the resume and application have and from there put it in a searchable if not indexable format. There has to be some methodology of qualifications that dismisses applicants. There is no way that the above example could have interviewed all applicants, a half, a quarter or even an eighth. It does not take that long for some staffer or intern to simply hold CTRL and F and enter these search queries.

Regardless of academic achievement and employment experience, <u>*a resume should above all else infer effort*</u>. There are people with decades of experience that cannot describe what they do. There are Ph.D.'s that are not working but yet keep publishing (how does that work?). As a professional, you should be showing a continuance of training and development. It can mean training seminars, knowledge of regulations, industry standards and practices, having the ability to work both with and for staff and other organizations and so forth. Otherwise, you might suffer from what many call the "plateau effect" that you reached a point where you stopped rising but are not sinking either. You should never show a failure to having the ability to learn, adapt and grow.

Conclusion

In conclusion we should understand that a resume is an evolution. By that I mean that gradually it will get better exposure for your talents, abilities and education. Learning how to articulate yourself in the written word is great skill even beyond drafting a resume. The more you know about describing yourself the more you know to adapt that to other skills. In some sense it is like a puzzle because not everyone knows how to describe themselves. The best way is to gradually develop.

Websites mentioned:

Diffnow.com

This site can look at text inputs, file uploads and websites to see what the differences are between text documents. If information you found may have changed this can go character by character to determine what the change was.

Jobscan.com

This site can scan a resume and scan a job telling you specifically what is missing and what is common. They allow a certain number free but then charge.

Resume Examples

Let us look at some examples of what is a bad, good, better and best resume. These are all based on actual resumes. Starting in that order. Remember that all resumes are a form of evolution. Nobody starts out with a fantastic resume illustrating everything because chances are if you are really young you might not have that much to put down. But at the same point it is not always what you say it is how you say it. If this book is to infer anything it is that you should be able to explain yourself in terms that are understood by the employer so that way they do take you seriously and see you as one of their own.

Bad Resumes

Jane Doe
123 Main St
Any City USA, MA 02301
Home: 555-555-5555
Cell: 555-555-5555

Objective
Seeking to obtain a rewarding and challenging Customer Service position with a growth- oriented company that promotes a team environment and reaching the highest possible standards.

Qualifications Summary
- Extensive knowledge of principles and processes of providing customer and personal services, including customer needs assessment, meeting quality standards for services, and evaluation of customer satisfaction.
- Expert in the structure and content of the English language, including the meaning and spelling of words, rules of composition, and grammar.
- Very attentive, giving full attention to customers, taking time to understand the points being made, asking questions as appropriate, and conveying empathy.
- Outstanding communication and interpersonal skills.

Education
Any town High School   High School Diploma (June 1972)

Work Experience

Flight Attendant: October 1988 - June 2017, Southwest Airlines, Any City, MA

Provide personal services to ensure the safety and comfort of airline passengers during flight.
Greet passengers, verify tickets, and serve food and beverages.
Announce and demonstrate safety and emergency procedures such as the use of oxygen masks, seat belts and life jackets.
Answer passengers' questions about flights, aircraft, weather, travel routes and services, arrival times and life jackets.
Assist passengers in placing carry-on luggage in overhead, garment, or under-seat storage.
Guide passengers while entering or disembarking the aircraft
Attend preflight briefings concerning weather, altitudes, routes, emergency procedures, crew coordination, lengths of flights, food and beverage services offered, and a number of passengers.
Check to ensure that food, beverages, blankets, reading material, emergency equipment, and other supplies are aboard and are in adequate supply.
Collect money for meals and beverages.
Conduct periodic trips to the cabin to ensure passenger comfort and distribute reading material, headphones, pillows, playing cards and blankets.

Critique

Well for starters there is not anything really specific here. All this really says is this person was a flight attendant for thirty years. The education is based on high school which frankly should be removed given it is nearly forty years later. "In adequate" is one word. A simple check would have solved that issue. Being a native speaker of a language is fine but it is generally assumed that you would know English having graduated from high school and been a flight attendant for so long. Furthermore, why is there an objective here? Of course, they know you want the job you are applying to why else would you be applying? Also, past tense should be used here.

Bob Jones

Elm Avenue,

Des Moines IO, 50301

(617)555-1212

Summary of Qualifications

- Customer Service
- Organized
- Strong Leadership Skills
- Teamwork
- Motivational Skills
- Results Driven
- Computer Skills (MS Office)
- Detail Oriented

Work Experience

Bank of America:

Assistant Manager
08/2006 - Present

- Provide unrivaled customer service to ensure our customers receive the best possible in customer service standards
- Build trust and credibility by listening and understanding customer needs

- Provided subject matter expertise for new and existing associates
- Deliver 360 degree coaching during evaluation sessions
- Provide feedback for associates on a daily basis to ensure that they meet monthly metrics
- Handle escalation customers and provide resolutions
- Responsible for the Banking Center in an event where the manager is not present

The Limited Co:

Sales Leader
11/2003-08/2006
- Achieved monthly sales goals established by retail store and contributed to increased annual revenue
- Shared best practices with associates to improve performance and increase sales
- Balanced sales associates cash registers on a daily basis and made daily cash deposits
- Utilized security procedures during opening and closing the store each day
- Responsible for the operation of the store in manager's absence
- Coordinated and performed inventory of the store every 6 months

Achievements
- Consistently achieved Top Performer Award during 2008-2010
- Received Global Recognition

- Make a Difference Award Winner

Critique

Where do I start? First and foremost, there is so much in the way of blank space here that I would assume a third of the page is blank. Why is the address highlighted in yellow? What purpose does that serve? Global recognition? From what exactly? Ok, he did inventory. How many items were in the department or the store itself? The qualifications of skills are very limited in scope. How many customer accounts were managed? Was this business, residential or both? "Escalation customers" is a pretty generic term. What problems were specifically "solved"? In banking, there could be a wide range varying forms of fraud especially given the collapse of the housing and credit markets in 2008. Citing regulations illustrates knowledge; not doing it shows the opposite.

Do you like the book so far?
If so please consider leaving a review.
Reviews help make improved revisions.

Good Resumes

Patty Reirdon

42 Plain Road (C) 617-555-1212
(H) 781-555-1212
Boston, MA 02370

A talented and accomplished Business and Administrative professional with extensive experience.

Outstanding verbal and communications skills
Able to multi-task

Able to oversee all aspects of office operations   Strong background in business management

Proficient in Microsoft Office
Able to train and supervise personnel

Hard working detail oriented
Able to develop policy and procedures

Professional Experience

Christian Academy, Boston, Massachusetts
Director of Development, 2008-August 31, 2013
- Created a strong and successful development program through annual giving, stewardship of donors and major events.
- Created marketing and recruitment campaigns as well as all press releases and publicity
- Created and maintained alumni and donor databases
- Wrote and managed all correspondence.

- Planned and directed all cultivation, fundraising and donor events
- Researched and wrote grants to support the general operating budget.
- Managed several projects at a time responsible for recruitment and management of volunteer and intern staffing.
- Oversee department budget and created a three to five year strategic financial forecast.
- Provided support for the Regional Director and Board of Trustees administratively through preparation of materials for board meetings, correspondence, research, event planning and minutes of sub-committees.

Blue Cross & Blue Shield of Massachusetts, Boston, Massachusetts
Member Service Representative, 2006-2007
Provided outstanding customer service in a fast paced, highly structured call center. Advised customers regarding policy and benefit information for multiple health plans, Investigate and resolve member inquiries through correspondence and research.

Holy School Boston, Massachusetts, 1999-2006
Director of Advancement
Responsible for the creation and management of a successful advancement program including overseeing the development of donors, all events, budget, and annual campaigns.

Rockland Foundation, Rockland, Massachusetts

Development Coordinator, 1989-1999

State Street Bank, North Quincy, Massachusetts
Officer 1985-1991

Education
BA in Political Science with a concentration in Public Administration
Bridgesea State College, Bridgesea, Massachusetts-1982
Certification in Paralegal Studies

Stonehill College, Easton, MA-1987

Professional /Civic Organizations
Board Member-Needy Nonprofit.
Board Member-A local mission Anytown USA
ACAAP Support Staff Distinguished Service Award Winner
Member Chamber of Commerce
Past Vice-Chairman Anytown Board of Selectmen
Past Chairman Anytown Capital Planning Committee
Past Treasurer RLF Foundation

Critique

Well, this is a good resume although it can be stronger. I do not think that going back to the 1980's would be advisable but there is a fair amount here that can be expanded upon. She is selling herself short. "Able to oversee all aspects of office operations" Name them as that helps significantly. If you are in the area of receiving donations talk about the amounts and what was used. Raiser's Edge software by Blackbaud is a major piece of software that could be emphasized here. The board work is great but the resume seems so focused on donors that it really should start talking about amounts and from what organizations. This screams out for some form of a deliverable that would have been provided to a board of directors. If she expanded this and included that the annual reports be available upon request it would hit it out of the park.

Better Resumes

LORNA CARNIGN

32 Billford Square Marshland, Mass 02050 D@gmail.com
(781) 555-1212 (cell)

SUMMARY PROFILE

Results oriented professional with career experience and a proven record of success in real estate, sales, marketing, purchasing and customer service. Excel in positions demanding exceptional communication, organization and interpersonal skills. Reputation for exceeding expectations, resolving tough problems conducting needs analysis. Effective in converting strategies into specific actions, making decisions and communicating priorities. Diligent, high-energy and a talent for fact finding.

CORE COMPETENCIES

§ Sales, Marketing and Customer Service	§ Business and Client Development	§ Vendor Relations
§ Communications and Networking	§ Training, Teaching, and Mentoring	§ MS Software and Bookkeeping Skills
§ Maintaining Customer and Client Relations	§ Contract Negotiations	§ Leadership and Staff Development

EXPERIENCE

Real Estate and Sales
- Procured 95% of listings through continuing strong ability to meet challenges and procure market share of inventory
- Strong marketing concepts and proper sale techniques produced almost 100% of properties sold
- Produced schedules for office personnel on monthly basis minimizing absences and no coverage.
- Effective communication skills resulted in training new associates in all aspects of real estate sales.
- Thorough knowledge of software applications in Real Estate and marketing of properties.
- Knowledge of legal language in purchase and sale of real estate secured ability to draft contract language.
- Consistent team player recognized with company award for exceptional service to colleagues.

- **Customer Service and Purchasing**
- Build and maintain a strong and lasting relationships with vendors, clients, and builders
- Purchased materials necessary for day to day operation of shipyard and various construction materials for ships..
- Successfully negotiate contract prices and secure lower costs which resulted in receiving Minority Business Award.
- Negotiate, renegotiate, and administer contracts with suppliers, vendors, and other representatives

- **Teaching**
- Taught 6th-8th grade students in both contained and mainstream classrooms. Organized student planners, attended classes to monitor and contain behavior. Effective at reaching teacher goals resulting in multiple call backs to cover classroom
- Motivated students to have positive outlook on education. Positive motivation reduced absences of students by at least 40 %.
- Substitute teacher for Grades K-8 as well as classroom aide for grades K-12. Understand and teach the curriculum left by the regular teacher; learned and effectively taught a wide variety of subjects with literally 5 minutes to prepare.

EMPLOYMENT HISTORY

Real Estate Agent and Notary, Jack Estate & Co. Duxbury, MA and West Weymouth, MA
    1993-Present

Tutor, Adaptive Learning Program- Substitute Teacher/ Aide, Town of Seafield- School Department
    2002-2009

Buyer/Purchasing, General Dynamics –Quincy Shipbuilding Division, Quincy, MA

EDUCATION

BS, Business Administration & Management, Salem State College, Salem, MA

CERTIFICATIONS PROFESSIONAL SOCIETIES

Massachusetts Professional Real Estate License

National and Massachusetts Association of Realtors

Massachusetts Certified Realtor

Plymouth and South Shore Association of Realtors

Massachusetts Notary Public

National Notary Association

Critique

Now this one really works well. Although I would not totally agree with using a summary the experience section is where this excels. But then there are some issues. Are you really going to bring up material that is twenty or so years old? While the experience in real estate is solidly affirmed the purchasing, portion happened long ago. In fact, it does not list when it occurred so there could be so much in regulations and laws that one might disregard that without some form of credentials and training.

Debby Sousa
Telephone (508) 555-1212 *E-mail:*
abc123@yahoo.com

SUMMARY OF QUALIFICATIONS

Ø Computer literate in Word, Excel, PowerPoint, and Data Entry

Ø Strong work ethics-Dependable-Highly Self Motivated-Trustworthy

Ø Patient-Understanding and Calm-Able to work in fast paced environments

Ø Train, supervise and mentor-Follow through-Multi-task

Ø Work well independently as well as part of a team-Productive

Ø **Computer Skills** word, Excel, Power Point, and data Entry

Ø **Bilingual English / Portuguese**

PROFESSIONAL EXPERIENCE
National Accounts Manager
    2013-Present
Coastal Fire & Ventilation Babylon, NY
Schedule annual inspections with national accounts. Make Accounts Receivable calls. Answer phones and direct calls to appropriate person.

Housekeeping
    2012-2013
Clean Group Facilities/ Royal Taber Nursing Home Hudson, NY
Clean and organize resident's rooms.

Volunteer File Clerk
    2012-2012

Department of Transitional Assistance, Pittsfield, MA

Pull and organize files, create new records as necessary. Place materials into storage receptacles, such as file cabinets, boxes, bins, or drawers, according to classification and identification information.

Clerical/Data entry
2009-2009
Youth Build Great Barrington, MA
Responsible for processing applications. Entering new applicants into data base and filed when necessary. Worked with kids within the community by planting trees with the Mayor, fundraising, and cleaning up the city and abandoned lots by mowing the lawn, cutting shrubs, and picking up garbage. Created posters for upcoming events for the city. Revised and retyped handbook.

Manager
2001-2008
Sally Beauty Supply Co. Pittsfield, MA
Interviewed, hired, trained, and evaluated employees. Managed daily retail operation, planned work schedules Provided exceptional customer service to store customers and various businesses resulting in repeat business Handled sales, inventory taking, and cash receipt reconciliation Served as key holder, secured store, Received several merit increases, promotions and awards for meeting and exceeding sales goals, attendance and "The Eagles Eye" award for loss prevention.

EDUCATION

2012 Pscc
Online Course
Certificate: Responsible serving of alcohol

2011 Labaron's Beauty Academy
New Bedford, MA
 License: Cosmetologist

2009 Computer training Specialist II, Inc.
New Bedford, MA
Certificate: Computerized Office Program

1998 Gr New Bedford Reg. Vocational Technical High School   New Bedford, MA
Diploma/Certificate: Culinary Arts

Critique

I know that some people want to put everything on a resume and that is all well and good. Higher education often times advocates for people to become "well rounded". But there comes a time to focus. The oldest position is very well detailed but it appears after the third position that the descriptions have dropped considerably. If it is not pertinent to the job then do not put it there. Going from a degree in Culinary Arts to a computer certification in cosmetology and then an alcohol license is going all over the place. Also, the summary of qualifications is not that specific at all. There is potential here but it is going to have to come though.

These last ones are the best ones. These are ones that are straightforward, to the point and concise.

Mark Harold

123 Main St, Boston Ma (781-555-1212)
mark@msn.com

Recognized for strengths in written and verbal communications, planning; organizational development; budgeting and fiscal affairs; staff coordination; and working with economically and racial/ethnic diverse populations.

Education

Cambridge College
M.Ed.
Suffolk University   Project Management Certification
Massachusetts Department of Education   License 309663
Massachusetts Department of Education MTEL License (Pending)
Massachusetts Continuing Legal Education
Business & Commercial Law Studies
Northeastern University   Paralegal Certification

Professional Experiences:

Boys & Girls Clubs of Boston
   Dorchester, MA
Associate Director of Community Development
   (2012 – 2013)
Responsible for the direction of community relations, development and implementation of impacted programs e.g., summer camp licensing, inclusion and DOE food

service regulations; developing plans, events and projects to improve the overall relationship between the Dorchester community and BGCB by being the first point of contact for community groups and responding to the general public's request for information, rentals, leading community meetings and making presentations to the general public on plans and programs, partnering with community leaders to develop mutually acceptable community programs, directing and coordinating special community projects and observing issues through ongoing contact and information exchange with local officials, community leaders and other decision makers as well as interest groups.

Action For Boston Community Development (ABCD)
Boston, MA *Business Manager – Housing and Homelessness Department* (2011 – 2012) Responsible for the development of budget narratives for all departmental proposals following cost allocation and rate structure guidelines; complying with federal regulations and funding source requirements; review of all contracts for the department; preparing financial reports as required by the funding source; allocating internal charges and developing cost allocation plans; monitoring all departmental expenses; analyzing budget performance reports and payroll registers; preparing monthly journal entries; and similar tasks as required.

The Family Circle, Inc.
Dorchester, MA
Director of Education
(2005 - 2011)

Responsible for coordinating educational activities and managing such activities so that available resources were utilized efficiently; managed the physical details relating to education programs including scheduling of classes, instructor assignments, responsible for conference planning and activities; supervised educational staff; responsible for all aspects of speaker management for conferences; served as staff liaison to the Education Committee; development of the department budget and monitoring and managing the departmental income and expenses.

Director of Administration and Finance
(2005 - 2011)
Responsible for coordinating administrative activities, preparation and analyzing budget activity, audit/verify correctness of all invoices, reconcile and balance bank account at month-end, maintained group insurance and 401k retirement plans, processed company deposits and reconciled credit card transactions worked closely with the President in developing the administrative and financial aspects of the organization, developed a passionate team building infrastructure for clients and staff, preparation of weekly/monthly reports and created a commitment to improving client services as they relate to organizational goals and profitability.

Brandeis University (Sustainable International Development) Waltham, MA
Academic Services Administrator/Program Administrator
(2002 – 2005)
Developed new management standards for success of Executive Education Conferences and Workshops; developed new process for Reading Materials; designed

and facilitated Time Management Workshops for all incoming International students; responsible for Annual Cap Stone Event; counseled part-time MBA students; and provided tasks as required.

Harvard Law School (Human Rights Program)
Cambridge, MA
Administrator – Appointment
(2000 – 2002)

Administered and supervised all financial activities; managed the Program budget and a $4 million endowed budget; coordinated Advisory Council meetings; developed summer and winter intern programs; participated in student orientation; developed annual newsletter and factual publications; managed speaker panels and student sponsored conferences; and supported International Fellows.

Bingham Dana LLP
Boston, MA
Administrator
(1996 – 2000)

Responsible for managing legal practice for corporate partner and two associates; responsible for office procedures; maintained extensive client contact, handled sensitive/confidential situations; and participated in extensive domestic travel to close corporate transactions.

Community Colleges of Massachusetts
Boston, MA
Adjunct Faculty
(1986 - 1996)

Preparation and delivery of subject matter to students at Roxbury, Massasoit and Bunker Hill Community Colleges.

Cathedral High School
Boston, MA
Business Department Chairperson/Teacher
(1986 - 1988)
Reviewed Business Education curricula standards for middle and high school students; delivered classroom education to high school students; provided clinical observations and evaluations for department staff; provided formative evaluations, training and workshops; maintained department budget; provided monthly/annual reports, managed expenses and distributed monthly expenditure reports.

South End Adults at Cathedral
Boston, MA
Adult Education Teacher/Advisor
(1986 - 1988)
Preparation and delivery of education and counseling services to adult learners; curricula development; organizational development; instructional design and classroom management.

Volunteerism:
Youth Commission – Designed Mentoring Program
Vision Foundation – Board Member and Grant Develop

Critique

What can be said about this one? Well, it is very well written and gets to the point. Are there any long-winded sentences? No. Does it say roles and responsibilities? Absolutely. Some of this, in fact, might be too much but it clearly shows effort. This might be a bit over the top for a lower leveled position.

ESTER M. ROUND
12 Circle Road | Stoneland, MA | (781) 555-1212|
ER@ABC123.com

PT Accounting Assistant

Proactive office manager/bookkeeper with excellent computer, organizational and time management skills, dedicated to providing excellent customer service. Experienced Bookkeeper and office manager. Proficiency in accounting applications, and web design services. Proficiency in real estate software.

**QuickBooks / Outlook / Excel / Word / Quicken
PowerPoint / Publisher / Photoshop / Dreamweaver / Joomla**

Professional Experience

American eagle Technology Training Plus, Rockland, MA (Self-employed)   2007 – Present
Technology Specialist
- Created customized technology courses - Word, Excel, Outlook, Publisher, PowerPoint, iPad, Android
- Customized Web design - Joomla (open source) Dreamweaver CS6
- Developed brochures, business cards, marketing materials
- Social Media - Facebook pages for the individual or groups

America Five Technologies, Inc Braintree, MA
2012 - 2013
Office Manager/ Bookkeeper
- Created invoicing using Connectwise which is – IT automation software for help desk, ticketing, billing. Reviewed the Time sheets for each of the Technicians, Verifying the detail on what service they provided to the client, what the end result was, the job was completed in the correct amount of time Confirming the billing rates for that Job function and the rates per the Technician. Sent the invoice to the Client via Email. Then approved / rejected any expense associated with that job/ technician
- Selected / approved all invoices completed on a daily basis to be integrated with the accounting software QuickBooks. Once the Invoice have been imported into QuickBooks. These invoices were then manually entered into the Cash Flow spreadsheet
- Accounts Payable /Account Receivable - Cash Deposit / Collection Call for overdue accounts
- Credit card reconciliation / Bank reconciliation - multiple accounts
- Calculated Payroll for 10 employees

Sleepys Retail Store – West Roxbury
2011 - 2012
Office Manager /Bookkeeper

- Developed office procedures for sales staff to ensure quick, accurate reporting of information.
- Processed the Sales orders for the previous day into Quicken / Excel, verifying the payment /sales information
- Forwarded all balanced paperwork to Florida store to the company owner.

Performed bank reconciliation to online banking for multiple accounts after making the bank deposit.

- Customer Service - waiting on customers as needed

Health Care Store, Inc., Stoneham, MA
2008-2009
Account Representative
- Processed time sheets of Hairdressers for each salon in QuickBooks
- Verification of accuracy of the time /amount per function
- Data entry of payments – individual ATM deposits, individual daily credit card receipts, corporate deposits' recording on a weekly basis
- Balancing these to the invoices created in the processing of the time sheets
- Customer service for our clients and their families

UStaff, Quincy, MA
2006-2007
Payroll Bookkeeper
- Processed payroll for 1000-1200, importing time and rates using custom software

- Handled child support, IRS, state and federal tax payments
- Calculated Workers Compensation rates in Excel

Marcs Real Estate, Plymouth, MA
2003-2006
Bookkeeper
- Processed accounts payable /accounts receivable – for multiple companies / offices
- Calculated /called - ADP
- Maintained health ins., vacation/sick time tracking, employee files
- Balanced the bank reconciliations for 15 accounts (Sales, Escrow, Rental) Traveled to each office.
- Prepared escrow commission /Sales payments needed for closings
- Functioned as computer help-desk/system administrator for five offices
- Provided agent training in MS Office/ MLSpin for five offices as needed

EDUCATION
- Clark University – Computer Career Institute, Braintree, MA   2007.

Critique

It sounds like there is too much of an explanation for the first position but other than that it makes good points. Of course, the more specific it is the better the picture will be. By defining exactly what was done along with how it was done makes this the best of all of them.

Get the Job

Introduction

Congratulations, if you have followed the advice provided in Get the Interview you now have one. Ok, now what? Well, now you have the pass the second part of the gauntlet. If you not normally deal with people face facing this is going to be a bit of an awakening. Considering the stakes this is possibly the most important conversation you will have relative to the possibilities. Think about it for a moment. The largest events you could have purchased a house, earning a degree, marrying a spouse and raising a child all require much more than a general conversation. What you are about to do over the course of fifteen minutes to a few hours could yield you a stepping stone to a career, better pay and change your life. No pressure, right?

Prologue

My experience in this is grounded in having many interviews across the New England region. Interviewing skills are almost like learning to ride a bike. Eventually, you get comfortable with a sense of balance and you should be ready the next time. Of course, like a bike I would argue that "It is like learning how to ride a bike again" as expectations and standards change. This book is to give you the confidence to interview well. The more interviews you go on the better you will get at it. Sounds simple but you really do not want to go on many interviews given the work you just did to get this one. If you are well focused and to the point, you should be able to advance to a second interview and then hopefully the job.

There is almost a certain art to this. The back and forth, the body language, being able to answer a question in different ways all contribute to the way how you and they will be perceived. An interview is literally talking your way into a job but you have already been vetted by the resume. They know you have most of the qualifications but do not just tell them that was the resume, show them you are qualified.

Chapter One: The Interview

The interview process has to be one of the most grueling experiences that one may have in their life. To be questioned by a group of people that you do not know on a variety of questions is not an everyday occurrence. It can be intimidating, to say the least. Making it harder to understand is that there are no set rules about the process. Take for example the time one should be. I have had interviews as short as fifteen minutes and as long as two hours. Some employers will have you meet department heads while others might restrict that for the second interview. It might help to look up how long people have been in their positions as that might provide how long it has been since they have hired people. Employers with small departments with long longevity are more apt to fit here. Larger employers that higher significant numbers of temporary employees and part-time staff are more likely to be used to interviewing.

Make sure to ask prior to the interview as to who is interviewing you (pay attention to the titles) and how many people. There are huge differences between interviewing with a few people versus a potential grilling of a dozen. Long ago that happened to me. One by one each applicant was called in and it did not feel like an interview but rather that I was on trial. Not two, not five, not ten but FIFTEEN people were questioning me at the same time! It was a bit provoking and one applicant actually got into a shouting argument with one of the interviewers! You want to keep composure as much as possible. She said it would not reflect on her getting the position (she was wrong). At the same point nine months later, the salary for that position dropped by about fifteen percent!

Of course, you want to "Dress for success" and this means having a clean image. Formal attire is usually assumed to be the norm. Dress slacks and shirts for men and for women a blouse with slacks or a skirt should be fine. Having said that though there can be a situation where it just might not fit. People from Silicon Valley have told me that men's ties are no longer expected. Tattoo policies might vary but I would suggest that if you have them in your arms to wear a long-sleeved shirt. Larger earrings should be avoided. Do not go in with any form of perfume or cologne. Even if it does smell nice if an interviewer is allergic to it the interview would end shortly. If you are sick reschedule for a time when you are better. There is no reason to have an interview while sick because you might spread it to others, might not sound and look as good and it just is not professional.

You want to remain calm not just during the interview but also prior. I had an interview where I was so pumped I decided to claim the stairs rather than take the elevator to the interview room. It was four flights of stairs and needless to say I was pretty long winded once I arrived. But from their perspective, they just saw this tired applicant appear. Hold your energy for later this is a marathon, not a race. That reminds me if they offer you water, by all means, take it. That can allow you to get an opportunity to pause without it seeming awkward or jarring.

If you are doing an online interview check your equipment the day before. By equipment I mean not just the camera but the lighting, the internet connection and any software that might be used for the job. Some of this goes back to Photography 101. If you are using natural light or a lamp make sure it is not so bright that you are visible and there is no glare. At one point I was asked to lower the brightness so I lowered the shade. It lowered alright, it fell off! Thankfully this was before the interview, not during. Telephone interviews can often be used if distance or the weather is a factor. I strongly recommend a quiet area and would even recommend having it in front of a mirror if possible. That way it mimics that you are talking to someone face to face even when that really is not the case. As with online interviews make sure there are no distractions. If it is a smart phone putting it in airplane mode might be recommended. You cannot allow for any distractions, from the start to end the focus should only be on communicating the interview.

It is not that uncommon for employers to ask for writing samples or tests. If so the right software and version. If they send you a Word 2010 document with edits and your version is earlier you can be at a disadvantage. This is not to suggest you need the newest and greatest technology but if they ask for work samples or projects you should be able to deliver.

Interviews can be like snowflakes, no two are exactly alike. Remember you are interviewing them as much as they are interviewing you. Long ago I had a second interview where the process went off the tracks so much they came off as extremely unprofessional. The conversation devolved into some camping expedition in the south-west and the interviewers did not even work for the employer! Needless to say, it was not surprising to find that the department dissolved which eliminated the job I applied for and the one above it. There are also no rules about how long an interview should be. There are arguments about a half hour but I have had some that were as long as two hours or as short as fifteen minutes. Not everyone talks at the same speed and not all interviews have the same amount of people. There was one I had where it was a dozen applicants one by one given a half hour and then done and others where it was just a casual one interview a day approach. Each market is different depending on its requirements and the labor pool that applies.

You do not want to come into an interview process cocky but at the same time, you want to be prepared. Understand what their backgrounds are, what the roles, rules, and responsibilities of the position are and where it is going. Being competent is nice but you have to be motivated to do the job. Be prepared for giving examples of going the extra mile, achieving objectives similar to the job description. Give examples of where you had to persuade and motivate others to achieve results this can be a strong indicator of them of long-term success. Explain your areas of competency and provide strong evidence. By that, I mean showing well-developed skills and aptitude.

Here are examples of common interview questions to answer:

- Why do you want to work here? Go back to your background
- Why should we hire you? This is blunt but honest.
- Why do you want *THIS* job so badly? Again, this is blunt but honest
- Why do you want to work for us? You have to answer with examples of research. You want to show attention to what has happened to them. It could be a significant increase or decline, a merger or spin-off, a policy change etc.
- What makes you think you can work here? Again, this is blunt but this should be answered with credentials.
- Give me a story/Tell me a time you.... This one wants work examples that want to be relevant to that job.

- What are your greatest strengths? - This should be obvious
- What are your greatest weaknesses? - This can be an opportunity to be honest but highlight. If it is a finance job you can say you are not artistic etc.
- What would your current/last employer have to say about you? Be honest.
- Why do you want to leave your current position? Do not ever bad mouth a prior employer. Say something positive that shows you are growing like "I would like more responsibilities" or "A position like this would be the next step"
- Can you describe any conflict you faced? Who was it with and how did you resolve it?
- Can you give me an example of where you demonstrated initiative?
- Of all the things you have accomplished in your career, what stands out as most significant? Can you explain that in detail?
- What are the three or four biggest challenges you had to overcome?
- If you were to get this job, how would you go about solving _____?

You have to be prepared to answer such questions to get a second interview and certainly must deal with them to get a job offer. Remember there is nothing personal about these questions as they are usually asked from everyone. If you show some immediate facial response it is going to give a bad impression. Appearing confused is not a good attribute in this process or any process for that matter. Some might ask how they can practice without actually being in an interview. To that, I would answer going to Toastmasters and watching videos where people are questioned. Content I would recommend would be Shark Tank, Question Time from the BBC, Intelligence Squared and town and city hall proceedings where committees and board are questioned regularly.

In recent history there has been stories about very odd questions most notably from tech companies. For example "How many ping pong balls can fit into a 747?" If you are asked such questions what they are looking for is not an exact number but a thinking methodology. If there are any illegal questions such as mentioned earlier in chapter two in the prior book the best is to avoid them. At the same point, there are some employers that lately have established reputations for having extremely odd questions. "How many ping pong balls can fit into a 747?" is not really a relevant question. But if it gets a methodology of thinking that is what they are really looking for. If you get asked for something like this break it down so it can be done. If you can explain your thinking pattern that can better reflect them how you can deal with other situations.

Interviewing for a job that is different from what you currently do can be intimidating. Break down what you do at work and what remedies and any issues you deal with. Is it staffing, training, procurement, planning, marketing, board governance issues, IT etc. You would be surprised how similar employers can be to one another. They might call a process by a different name but the basics are still the same. Sometimes think of it the way how PC and Apple products are sold. Apple tends to use different words to imply their products are different but yet they do the same thing. Apple Airport is a wireless router and the Lightning is like a USB connection etc. I have seen employee documentation forms called Employee Action Forms (EAF) that list whenever a change has happened. Hiring, termination, name change, full-time equivalency (FTE) status change, compensation, time off etc. In the public sector there are quote forms and on the Federal side what is called Independent Cost Estimate forms (ICE). The point being is that much of the time you are doing the same operations they are doing but you might not know how to properly articulate it. The more you appear to say and do the things they do you will appear to them more as an employee and less of an applicant.

You must appear confident. There is also a strong difference between being prepared and having a canned memorized response. Speak like you are in a normal conversation. If you accidentally talk faster or louder it will make you look unprofessional. A good example of this is if you use GPS software. The general default voices of text to speech that sounds quite robotic. Actual downloadable voices are specific to accents and sound much more human. It is also much better to take your time and remove any "Um's" and "Ah's" as pausing to think can pay off. I know people on a professional level that is great at writing (his CV is about eight pages and gets published every few months) but he is terrible at speaking. He once said "Um" during a presentation about six times in a row. It was a hard struggle but I managed to keep my laughter to myself!

You should also answer the question and not waver dancing around the issue. Senator Ted Kennedy was famously asked in 1979 "Why do you want to be president?" This televised event actually interrupted the nightly news and he clearly had years of experience in the US Senate. Coming from one of the most famous political families in the world one would assume he would be articulate and to the point. The results, however, were nothing but. Senator Edward Kennedy talked for about two minutes but did not answer specifically why he wanted to be president. It will be argued about how much it played into him losing the primary to President Carter for generations. Subsequently, the renomination process for the Democratic party has not been challenged since (38 years as of this writing). Truth be told if you get asked a question it helps to answer it! The video itself be found here: www.youtube.com/watch?v=TDh2iKzBh4E

You must always look interested and pay attention. To deviate might appear poorly. Remember it is one thing to waste your time but if the interview is a waste of their time it could establish a bad reputation. Getting multiple departments to schedule time is not easy. Interviews are not always a priority and frankly, departments have other things to do. Factor in weekends, holidays, shift differences, vacations and sick time and one can easily see why it this process is long. Another example can be seen when in a 1992 town hall debate President George HW Bush looked at his watch. Was he tired? Bored? Who knows but it stood out because it reflected poorly. Did he think he was late for something else? Who knows? Likewise, do not be distracted and do not distract yourself. If there is a fly in the room resist the instinct to look at it and turn your cell phone off. At the same point make sure there is nothing *you* are doing that is distracting. If something is shiny or blinks somehow it would be best to avoid wearing it. It is hard to not stare at things especially if it acts as an invitation. It is for that reason you should never wear anything with words on it. Words are meant to be read. A tie with some funny saying, a tie clip from your old college frat/sorority or some belt with your initials should not be worn.

Like the resume, you should combine your experience of working, education, internships and perhaps volunteering to illustrate why you are qualified. Layering and framing are where this gets very powerful. If you know event planning and billing that can help show you can work with coordinating with companies. Here are a few examples. If you know IT with music formats and played in a band that might help with a music company. Another could be if you learned to cook while in high school but also know how to service people with ailments from volunteering at a soup kitchen. That might help in interviewing for a director of a senior center.

You can get people to agree or not agree on an issue for different reasons. Take for example if a factory is looking to expand operations in a community. Proponents will advocate that this expands the number of jobs and that can lower crime rates. The economy in the area would then benefit from the competition and higher wages. Opponents would advocate that pollution and traffic will lower their quality of life. The best way for the factory to maximize approval is to think of every and any possible negative aspect and how to get people to bring in more approval. If it is constructed at night to provide the hours and perhaps forms of insulation of sound and light. If could mean showing filtering systems that prevent airborne particles from being emitted. It could also mean showing the sponsorship of other businesses and events to counterbalance anything perceived as negative.

Here is an example of ends and means with opposition and selling. I know of a small plaza that received a one-million-dollar grant from the Recovery Act. Everyone agreed about the project but they did not agree with the timing. The liquor store said it could not start November or December because that is a peak for the holiday season. Then the pizza shop said they could not start in January or February because that is their busy time for the NFL playoffs and Super Bowl. Then a flower shop said they could not do March or April due to the Easter flower season! At that point, they put the flower shop in a trailer for the duration of demolition and construction. At no point could anyone tolerate a pause for a half year just because three businesses protested the project start date. What is vital to one group is not always to another.

What can you do that is better, cheaper or faster? Tell them how you can perform for them. Please do not say something that might sound meaningful or symbolic at first but at a second glance appears utterly stupid. How many used car salesmen have said "This car is going to take you places" well any car (should) be able to take you places! Some roles are more for turning a place around.

You want to be able to consider all of the roles of what is involved. If you get asked a question about operations and are able to show that you can anticipate what other parties' do that relates a bit to game theory. Game theory is a pretty wide-ranging through multiple disciplines. The topic itself is well beyond the context of this book. If you are interested in a comprehensive introductory book I would highly recommend Game Theory: A Critical Introduction by Shaun Hargreaves-Heap and Yanis Varoukakis.

Of course, in an interview, you have the opportunity to ask questions after they are finished. Take this opportunity very seriously because they will be looking to see your interests. Avoid asking soft questions that have answers you can easily find on their website or local media. Some might suggest that asking such questions would put them at ease and allow them to say things more freely. This is a job interview, not a date. Powerful questions can make them view you as a serious candidate that wants the job.

Here are examples of powerful interview questions to ask:

- What is the history of the position? Again, they have to be honest about this as you are not

specifically saying why or how the last person left but having a sense of duration and any increase or decrease would be a great benefit.
- If I were to start here in two weeks what would day one look like? This does a few things. It puts you a bit at ease because no employer in their right mind is going to say the job is chaos for their probationary period. They have to be honest and if they cannot describe what is going on it would reflect poorly. It also puts you inside their mind *already* working.
- What would you say would be my biggest challenge here? - This might sound like you are a bit full of yourself but this establishes a few things. You are serious about the job and they are serious about it existing. Remember not all tasks are made into outright jobs. Between outsourcing, automation and merging it with another there *had* to be some reason why it was planned the way it is.
- When should I hear back? - Save this one for the end but do not **_ever_** leave without asking that question. You could have the best interview ever but if you do not know when you will hear back your anxiety will be mind-numbing. The more effort you put into getting the interview the higher likelihood you should ask.

There is also a bit to say about if they ask for projects. Work/writing samples generally make sense to get a feel for how someone can document their work. Some of these projects are just a way of simply obtaining free labor. None the less you should take them seriously and do your best. This could be in the form of a presentation, a spreadsheet, a report etc. If it involves a presentation it can be hard to judge what their office may be like. Ask them what formats they want because again like the resume if it is not the same versions it might not totally appear the same way. Go over what it is the night before and make sure all text is legible. Long ago while in college a classmate made a Powerpoint with orange letters and background. None of the text showed up because he did not change the colors at the start!

Of course, there can be multiple interviews depending on the employer. Generally, from my experiences after a second interview, a decision is made although some might take three. However, I have heard from a friend that worked at a major international nonprofit that they would have as many as eight! This all depends on the size and scope of the bureaucracy.

Conclusion

Although sending an email thanking those that interviewed you can be nice there is a caveat. When sending, send it to those that *actually* have the hiring capability. Thanking people that have nothing to do with the process is not a good use of time and might actually make you appear that you do not know their structure. When I was in third grade the sciences held my interest and I wrote to Edmund Scientific requesting a catalog. I hand wrote the request but had no clue who it was supposed to get to specifically. *FIVE* years later I received that catalog. My point being is it was handwritten with no real direction at that company. It went down a rabbit hole. It would be nice to assume that everyone that interviewed you had some sway but that is not always the case. If a consensus is needed to interview view that does not mean that everyone there is relevant to the end result. If the employer deals with unions sometimes ia union representative might be there to observe but has no say.

Waiting for results can be very stressful but remember this is not always easy for them either. Coordinating people around multiple schedules is not easy. Factor in a budgetary process, the weather, potential politics, needs of departments and this process slows.

No matter how good you felt the interview went, do not consider the job a sure thing until a job offer is in your hand. If the economy has taught us anything in the past ten years is that budgets can be cut. This is not as common today but if the job is grant funded that might be a possibility depending on political and budgetary swings.

If you did not get the job there are others out there. On a side note, it might help to look up who specifically had it and looking up their credentials on LinkedIn. That way you can see what they had that was the difference.

Also, keep in mind just because someone was hired does not mean they will stay at the job. I have personally seen some that were hired potentially by mistake or had a time crunch. Not everyone that gets in can move up. If you have ever read the Peter Principle you know what I am referring to. There is also much to be said in that when people move up to another job they move out of another job. Sometimes you can tell openings months ahead of time simply because a job might not have that many applicants. I know of a funny story where there was an opening and an Ivy League graduate applied and got in. Well, this person intimidated the assistant to the point where she actually left! Ironically, the Ivy grad did not even work one day but had another offer. This created two openings instead of one.

There is an old saying that the worst place in the Olympics is not bronze but silver. Why silver? Because if you were left out of gold by a small amount then that amount is going to be hard to forget about. Whereas if you were bronze you will always know and understand you needed more to get gold. It was also said by Thomas Jefferson "Mankind are more disposed to suffer, while evils are sufferable than to right themselves by abolishing the forms to which they are accustomed". Even back then the idea of being in a comfort zone was understood.

If you liked this book please provide a review.
Reviews help provide funding to enable more content to be published.
Coming soon Adult Budgeting 101.

Recommended readings on this subject include:

60 Seconds and You're Hired! By Robin Ryan

www.amazon.com/60-Seconds-Youre-Hired-Revised-ebook/dp/B00XIYG6US/

and

Knock'em Dead Job Interview by Martin Yate

https://www.amazon.com/Knock-Dead-Job-Interview-Interviews-ebook/dp/B00J08H0QK/

www.ingramcontent.com/pod-product-compliance
Lightning Source LLC
Chambersburg PA
CBHW070202230526
45471CB00002B/789